YOUR CHARACTER FROM
THE STARS

Describes the general principles and physical
characteristics associated with each sign of the
zodiac, and reproduces text of a lecture delivered
by author to the Astrologer's Convention
regarding the planet Uranus, 'teacher and guide
of mankind'.

YOUR CHARACTER FROM THE STARS

By

T. MAWBY COLE

With a Foreword by
VERA W. REID

SAMUEL WEISER INC.
734 Broadway, New York, N.Y. 10003

First published 1968
Second Impression 1970
Third Impression 1971
Fourth Impression 1973
Fifth Impression 1975
Sixth Impression 1977

ISBN 0 85030 032 0 (UK)
ISBN 0 87728 096 7 (USA)

*Made and Printed in Great Britain by
Weatherby Woolnough, Wellingborough
Northants, England, NN8 4BX*

CONTENTS

FOREWORD

by VERA W. REID

T. Mawby Cole was a truly great astrologer. He had not only an intuitive approach and a deep insight into astrological principles, but also a very considerable practical experience in delineation.

He devoted his life to the study of astrology and it would be true to say that he lived, thought and dreamed it. It came as naturally to him as the air he breathed. His knowledge of his subject was in every sense a part of himself which he delighted to share with others and to devote to their service. He was a born teacher whose sincerity of purpose never failed to carry conviction and to give practical help to those who sought his advice. His method was to discuss the horoscope, explain its meaning, and to indicate the purpose of events we are called upon to meet and deal with in the course of our lives.

The philosophy underlying his delineations was the subject of *Gods in the Making,* a book written in response to demands made by many people who had benefited through his teaching and were anxious to have an opportunity to study it more fully.

T. Mawby Cole planned to write a book on astrology "when he had time". Had he been able to do so he would undoubtedly have made a valuable contribution to astrology. As it was, his intention was not to be fulfilled, and he left only a collection of miscellaneous notes and articles, which make up this booklet. Amongst them was a series of descriptions of the twelve signs of the Zodiac together with the physical characteristics of each sign.

In 1941 T. Mawby Cole attended the Harrogate astrological conference, when he told those present that "events just staggering" would happen in the early hours

of May 11th. In his forecast he said that "whatever
influence comes about at this time will be no temporary
measure". Subsequently, on the night of May 11th, he
attended a meeting of the Group for Sacrifice and Service,
in the ballroom of a large house in Kensington. The meeting, which included prayers, hymns and periods of medita-
tion was timed to run from 1 a.m. until 5.15 a.m. and was
conducted by Dr. Bertha Orton (Gothian), an eye specia-
list and leader of the group in this country. T. Mawby
Cole had said that a "staggering" arrangement of the
planets would occur at "19 seconds past 5.15". This was
very near to the time when a bomb landed on the house,
killing fifteen and injuring twenty-seven of the sixty-odd
people present. Dr Orton and T. Mawby Cole were
among the dead.

Astrology was known as the Sacred Science to many
ancient peoples who held it to be the repository of all
knowledge and wisdom and to embrace all lesser sciences.
In view of this it may not be surprising to find that a
study of the subject may lead us far afield and bring to
us not only a deeper understanding of ourselves and our
friends but may also serve to remind us of our link with
the cosmos or greater whole of which we are a part.

The following notes on the twelve signs of the zodiac
describe the general principles associated with each sign
but, when studying them, it is well to remember that they
are no more than sign posts which each must learn to read
for himself. The extent to which the qualities of any one
sign are expressed by the individual depends upon more
than one factor. Thus although the sun sign corresponds
to the month of birth it is essential to bear in mind that
no one expresses the qualities of his sun sign only. A person
with his sun in one sign may, and often does, show more
clearly the influence of one or more other signs whose
influence depends not only on the month of birth but also
on the time of day, place and year of birth.

The birth chart or horoscope may be compared to the
face of a watch or clock each being divided into twelve

parts, the hour, minute and second hands of the time-piece being geared to the daily rotation of the earth on its axis and thus indicating the cyclic progression of time during the two periods of noon to midnight and midnight to noon respectively. In the birth chart each of the twelve divisions measures approximately 2 hours and like our time-piece indicate the 24 hour cycle of the earth's daily axial motion. The birth chart or horoscope has however many more "hands" than the time-piece and registers not only the axial motion of the earth but also the movements of many other cycles all of which take place against the background of the celestial zodiac. These cycles include the yearly rotation of the earth round the sun, the monthly rotation of the moon round the earth and also the greater and less cycles of the planets round the sun from the 248 year cycle of Pluto, the outermost planet, to that of Mercury, the innermost planet which rotates in a period of 88 days. Thus although the celestial zodiac forms the background against which the sun and planets of our solar system revolve it is easy to understand that the influence of those which are inhabited by the sun or planets is more evident than those that are, as it were, uninhabited. This applies particularly to the sign rising on the eastern horizon at the moment of birth and which is known as the rising sign.

Mr. Cole attached the greatest importance of this rising sign, likening it to the window through which we look out into the world and saying that the view thus obtained coloured our whole attitude to life. Again and again he urged his students to study the characteristics of the signs in order that they might be in a position to verify a given birth time or to establish it correctly when it was unknown. The first cry is considered by most astrologers to be the correct moment of birth and as this may not always be registered exactly either by the mother or by those attending to her, there is often confusion on this point, particularly as, in some instances, the difference of a few minutes may mean the transition of one rising sign to another. And so, if the moment of birth should prove to be incorrect the reading of a horoscope may be seriously distorted or given a faulty emphasis. For this reason Mr. Cole was always reluctant to draw up a horoscope or to discuss it until he had had the opportunity of meeting and talking with the person concerned in order that the moment of birth might be verified or if necessary corrected.

The position of the sun governing the essential or basic character, the moon the personality and Mercury the mental abilities are of course also of importance but their influence is not usually so readily discernible as that of the rising sign which governs the general appearance and the physical structure of the body.

1968   V.W.R.

ARIES ♈ *(1st House)*
THE RAM, SHEEP OR LAMB

March 21st to April 20th

Aries is a cardinal, fire sign ruled by Mars and is portrayed in the human race as force, energy, enthusiasm, idealism and activity, manifesting through all the three functions of man, physical, emotional and mental.

Hence Arians represent the active element in the community. They are the explorers, the breakers of new ground and are therefore known as pioneers. They have courage and enterprise; they live to take risks and usually face difficulties promptly and bravely. Being lovers of freedom and having an independent spirit they resent interference or restraint.

Arians are generous by nature and are willing to give freely of themselves and to devote time and money to any cause which arouses their enthusiasm. They seldom bear a grudge and are as ready to forget and forgive as they are to be hasty and impatient.

Since Arians are born leaders and good organisers, they are endowed with self-confidence and have a positive attitude towards life. Thus they are capable of filling positions of responsibility in which they can direct and manage others. They are masters rather than servants and it is difficult for them to function in a subordinate position.

They tend to become fanatical and absorbed in their own interests, but can inspire others with enthusiasm, specially as they are apt to consider it their duty to get their ideas widely accepted. They should, however, consider whether their ideas are really constructive and of universal value, or whether they are only derived from self-interest. In this way they will avoid expenditure of time and energy which could be more usefully employed in other directions. As others follow their initiative, it is important that they themselves do not make mistakes.

Although the work of an Arian is pioneering it is often only in the initiation of a scheme that they find their full expression. They should guard against the tendency to leave their schemes in mid-air, or of jumping into something new before the thing they have already attempted is launched.

Sometimes the attraction towards new thoughts and schemes is so strong that their enthusiasm and impulsiveness gets the better of them and then others have to complete what they have started. They would do well to work in partnership with someone who has practical ability and patience; ideas come to Arians in such rapid succession that much of their usefulness is lost through not being given to a practical person to work out.

Arians will rarely acknowledge defeat because they possess a strong will and a persistence and determination that are not easily discouraged. And, sometimes, when they meet with obstacles, material or spiritual, they are so engrossed in the fight against them, that they are unaware of their own suffering and so can win what to others would be a losing battle.

The spirit of an Arian is unquenchable. He is endowed with unusual powers of resistance and the ability to survive severe afflictions and to rise above grave misfortunes.

The hastiness and impulsiveness of Arians is shown both in their speech and writing. They do not stop to analyse their own statements nor even pause to register them on their own consciousness. They forget that if they themselves do not analyse, others do, and so when challenged with their previous statements they often deny that they made them.

Arians have a high regard for truth but often their idealism inclines them to exaggerate and to promise more than they can easily perform. They should think, and think hard, before making statements or promises, either written or spoken.

Arians are egoists and the one word they love is "I". It is always "I am" or "I am not". One of the most important lessons they have to learn is to give the other man a chance to express his opinions and to understand his point of view.

The Arian tendency to exaggerate arises from his desire for approbation and a sub-conscious urge to impress others with their qualities of leadership, for no matter what their circle of association may be, they want to be the outstanding figure in it. This is the reason why it is so difficult for them to acknowledge either to themselves or to others that they make mistakes. Yet they will be far more constructive if they realise that it is by our mistakes that we learn.

The fire of Aries is a spiritual force, dangerous yet purifying. As development proceeds, uncontrolled impulses are replaced by the inspiration of steady vision.

TAURUS ♉ *(2nd House)*
THE BULL OR OX

April 21st to May 21st

Taurus is a fixed earth sign and ruled by Venus. It is symbolised by the Bull whose characteristics are strongly portrayed in Taurians. They have strong bodies and are plodding, strong-willed and can be very stubborn. They are self-reliant and once they have accepted an idea they follow it with unswerving purpose.

In the quality of fixity lies one of the Taurian's greatest dangers. Thus, when an opportunity is offered to them, they may hesitate and then accept it when it is too late to profit by it. Again, because of their fixity they may continue to pursue an idea after all the virtue has gone out of it.

The symbol of the Bull marvellously portrays this characteristic. A bull will hesitate before he decides to attack but having once made up his mind, he puts his head down and charges straight towards his objective. If his victim side steps, he will fail to observe it and still rush on only to attack empty space.

Taurians are conservative and rather old-fashioned. They are fixed in their habits and find it easier to live in a rut than to accept new ideas or to venture forth towards anything new.

But, on the other hand, this Taurian fixity is of great value. It is for Arians to scheme and for Taurians to act. Their desire to accumulate possessions and wealth gives them the desire to produce. Were it not for the Taurian qualities the world of production would not come into being, and it is because Taurians love and seek possessions that they desire to produce and to conserve them.

The Taurian function in the collective is to transmute

the thought creations of others into physical manifestation. These people are excellent workers and reliable partners.

Ireland is ruled by Taurus and who does not know the value of an Irish navvy? When we think of the many repetitive and monotonous occupations, we may be thankful for the Taurians who have such great powers of patience and endurance. Particularly so since they often lack ambition and are content to make money for others rather than for themselves.

The influence of Venus, their ruler makes Taurians love ease, pleasure and comfort; they know how to enjoy possessions to the full. Speak to a Taurian about food and wine and you will find that the conversation will be most interesting. When he is not busy, he knows what a comfortable armchair is for and some Taurians in executive positions work very hard in armchairs.

The influence of Venus also makes a Taurian emotionally possessive. If Venus be in Taurus he will love but once for Taurians are faithful loyal and devoted friends.

The possessiveness of Taurus, however, is different from that of the opposite sign, Scorpio. Scorpio has the Mars element which develops into jealousy and strife, whereas Taurus has the Venus one which brings peace and happiness,

The Taurian's desire for peace is so strong that he will put up with a very great deal before he either complains or criticises. But should his peace be disturbed or his anger roused, he can then become like a roaring bull, self-willed, dangerous and stubborn.

Taurians can be deeply moved by sympathy and feeling, for they are ruled by their hearts rather than by their heads. Their feelings however tend to be repressed for they are reserved and may experience a difficulty in expressing what they feel. Because they are naturally secretive they know how to keep secrets.

Taurians are usually attracted towards the things of the earth, such as farming, mining, building, catering. They also make good masseurs and nurses, having great vitality themselves which they can impart to others.

In the higher expression of the sign, the Venus influence makes them idealistic. They like singing, music and the practical arts such as architecture. They are interested in pleasure and entertainment and as Taurus rules the larynx, this sign gives us the finest singers.

If, as we have already said, there is a purpose in the scheme of things which makes possessions of so much value in human development, then surely these possessions are to help man to become aware of himself in the objective world.

Now our first possession is the cells of our own body. It is not until we have a body that we can say "I am", for we must have a form in order to become conscious of other forms.

As in Aries we find the desire to be manifested, to seek new experiences, so in Taurus we find that which defines us and enables us to become conscious in the world of form. And having once established ourselves in the world, we seek to possess as much of it as possible; for in the contrast between what we own and what we lack lies the chief incentive which makes us more aware of ourselves.

This is the great mission of each one of us as human beings; first to become conscious of ourselves, to establish our individuality; then to become conscious of our duty to the collective. Then, having defined ourselves, we are able to understand the concrete world represented by Gemini, the sign following Taurus, and also the abstract world represented by Sagittarius, the sign following Scorpio.

But through Scorpio, the opposite and complementary sign ruling the eighth house of sensation and death, the Taurian realises that in the experience of sensation he must give up something of himself, while in death he loses even his first possession : the cells of his own body.

GEMINI ♊ *(3rd House)*
THE TWINS

May 22nd to June 22nd

Gemini is a mutable air sign ruled by Mercury. It is the first of the mental signs.

In Aries we have new beginnings, the desire to be manifested; in Taurus possessions through which we establish ourselves at the physical level.

In Gemini the mind begins to function and seeks to become related to the world of form. The mind must function through form for behind all material form there is mind, and it is on the mental plane that all things are created. The mental world is therefore the field of function for the Geminian.

It is in Gemini that the great dualities of life meet—spirit and matter, subjective and objective—for unless these two are united there can be no awareness.

In Gemini the mind seeks to become objectified, while in Sagittarius, its polar opposite, mind has become so firmly established that it can be used as a creative force.

The Geminian is mentally restless. He thirsts for experience and when it is not forthcoming he feels frustrated and unhappy. It must have been a Geminian who said "Variety is the spice of life" for the urge of the spirit allows him neither rest nor satisfaction. He constantly seeks but never finds what he is looking for. It is as though he realises that every experience has significance and so becomes over-anxious to gain as much experience as possible; a condition which explains the over-anxiety, restlessness and changeability of the Geminian.

The Geminian investigates the properties of matter and the phenomena of the concrete world. He delights in experiment and in everything about which he can reason and make comparisons. Thus under this sign we find the scientist who is attracted to all those branches of knowledge which seek to unite mind and matter.

Gemini rules commerce, also London and the U.S.A. While Sagittarius governs shipping and long-distance travel, Gemini governs that which is shipped, i.e. goods in circulation, short journeys and all forms of local transport.

Thus the Geminian is interested in communications and everything that lies close to his hand. He likes to handle things and can become a good craftsman. But if his hands are not occupied, they are extremely restless. It is he who gesticulates, taps with his fingers, fumbles in his pockets, rolls his bus ticket.

The Geminian goes through life in a hurry. He concentrates best when walking or travelling, for motion satisfies his physical restlessness and at the same time stimulates his mind.

All occupations demanding a quick response to the mental and physical worlds are attractive to the Geminian. For instance journalism attracts him, for there mind and matters are in constant interaction; or, again, advertising in which his mind can express itself in relation to commerce.

The Geminian is at his best in an emergency. In a moment of crisis he knows instinctively what to do and how best to do it.

He likes to write and to record his experiences. Many famous diaries are the work of Geminians. He frequently earns his living as a writer, secretary, librarian or clerk.

He can be clever in legal matters and makes a good public speaker though he is nervous when asked to speak without due preparation.

He enjoys reading and loves books because they help him to escape from a fixed environment. He feels that if he himself is debarred from the experiences he desires he can at least enjoy those of other people and in this way he is able to extend his awareness and general knowledge.

Gemini is a dual sign and duality is characteristic of

the Geminian. He often has dual experiences, follows two
occupations simultaneously, changes from one profession
to another while the main events of his life tend to be
repeated. He sometimes expresses the wish to be in two
places at once and likes to do as many things as he can at
the same time.

On account of his duality the Geminian has the faculty
of seeing both sides of a question and so is able to appreciate the other person's point of view. So much is this the
case that he is apt to suffer from indecision, to be hesitant
in making a choice or coming to a definite conclusion.

His inquiring spirit drives the Geminian from one
experience to another before the first has been assimilated.
Thus he is inclined to skim the surface and to leave many
things unfinished. This gives him the reputation of being
superficial and unless he cultivates concentration he may become a "Jack of all trades and master of none". He works
best in fits and starts but can accomplish a great deal if he
is left to do it in his own way and at his own time.

Mercury rules the nervous system and the Geminian
expends a vast amount of nervous energy. Anxiety and
worry can deplete his resources and may even seriously
lower his powers of resistance.

The Geminian is gifted, sensitive and highly strung. He
is however, mentally timid and apt to mistrust himself. He
suffers from nervousness which he usually manages to hide
under a bold front, but even when he tries to be aggressive
he feels inwardly uncertain and nervous.

The lower type of Geminian lacks persistence and is
inclined to be argumentative. When Mercury is afflicted
he wastes time in useless chatter.

The Geminian should cultivate concentration, avoid
having too many irons in the fire and learn to finish one
thing before he begins another. He should also learn how
to relax physically and mentally. When he begins to
understand his own motives he grows rapidly in self-know-
ledge and finds life not only more interesting but also
more worth while.

CANCER ♋ (4th House)
THE CRAB OR SCARAB

June 23rd to July 23rd

Cancer is a cardinal water sign and is ruled by the Moon.

Now the Moon has no light of her own but receives, retains and reflects light from the Sun. The element of water also reflects light and shade. It is these qualities of reception and reflection which are outstanding in Cancerians.

It is the power to receive and to reflect what they receive that gives to the Cancer type its marvellous memory. Also Cancerians are extremely sensitive to their environment. They can tune in to other people's moods and can sense an atmosphere, for they are constantly taking in and absorbing everything around them.

Many Cancerians have psychic powers and are able to practise psychometry. In this way they are able to obtain vivid impressions of past events associated with objects, places or houses. This faculty even if it is not consciously used, gives a unique quality to the memory of Cancerians.

It is perhaps for this reason that Cancerians have a natural interest in family traditions, ancient history and anything that pertains to the past.

Cancer is the sign that rules the fourth house which is associated with home and domestic affairs. And as it is at this point that the soul or emotional expression comes into being, we find another strong characteristic, that of feeling.

Feeling is so strong in Cancerians that it takes the place of reason. They select and reject according to their feelings for people and things, for they are closely linked with the soul plane, i.e. with the next set of vibrations to the physical.

It is this unconscious link with the emotional plane of soul that makes them so sensitive not only to physical impressions but also to abstract ideas. Very often in their conversation they astound others by expressing some provocative thought which has deep significance.

As we have already remarked some Cancerians have marked psychic powers but all at times seem to be overshadowed by or to have established a link with, the Universal Mind.

Cancerians are so sensitive that they often feel like a crab without its shell, defenceless and at the mercy of the elements. This causes them to hide their inner feelings and to present a mask to the world. As the Cancerian is so easily hurt himself he suffers in imagination at the thought of possible suffering he may have unintentionally inflicted on others. Thus at times he tends to magnify incidents and to worry over things which may be of little or no importance.

But in spite of this extreme sensitivity, because Cancer is a cardinal sign, a Cancerian will always retain his own identity, as opposed to the Piscean type which has a tendency to lose it. This ability to retain his selfhood and yet be sensitive makes the Cancerian a practical helper and sympathetic to the unhappiness of other people. You will more often find him sharing the sufferings of others than their joys.

Since, as we have said above, a Cancerian often wears a mask, he tends to live in a world of phantasy. He may even re-live the past over again, or, having an active imagination, he may day-dream about the present, in the manner of an author visualising his characters in his book. Sometimes much valuable time is wasted in imagining what might have happened yesterday or what may happen tomorrow. In this case the ideas are often far removed from reality.

In contrast to the negative day-dreaming of the unevolved Cancerian, the positive type has great creative power and through the exercise of visualisation and imagination can successfully materialise his thought creations.

As the Moon waxes and wanes so Cancerians change from one mood to another. Self-confidence is followed by timidity, courage by depression, serenity by explosions of irritability and then, perhaps a desire for forgiveness.

As the Moon fertilises and controls growth so Cancer represents the Mother and the maternal instinct. Cancerians, even the men, are always domesticated and like to "mother" people. Home and family means more to them than to those born under any other sign. And although the Moon gives a fondness for travel and change they cannot be happy without a settled background and never entirely break away from the ties of home and family.

One of the chief characteristics of the crab is to hold on, and we find Cancerians have this tendency. Tenacity may cause them to cling to an idea until they bring it to a successful conclusion, or, on the, other hand, they sometimes hold on when it would be wise to let go. This is another aspect of the maternal instinct which makes the mother reluctant to let her child go its own way. In the same way, Cancerians should let their thoughts go out into the Universe to find their fulfilment.

LEO ♌ (5th House)
THE LION OR HERCULES

July 24th to August 23rd

Leo is a fixed fire sign and ruled by the Sun. It is known as the royal sign and this characteristic is shown in the Leonian's kingly bearing, dignified manner and in his general approach to life.

The Leonian is a born ruler, and as Leo rules the heart, he rules with his heart as well as with his head. There is feeling and understanding in his leadership in contrast to the leadership of Aries which has more drive in it.

Leonians are born to be served and usually command service and attention without apparent effort, for they find it easier to give than to take orders.

Leonians are very proud. Their pride is easily wounded and they resent any affront to their dignity. Yet out of compassion they can sometimes forget their pride and are capable of outstanding acts of kindness and consideration. I have known a Leonian act as a servant to help a friend out of a difficulty and to go round begging clothes for someone who was down and out.

The great function of a Leonian in the collective is to develop and establish culture, for they are born with a natural distinction which can be recognised at a very early age. It is for this reason that the Leonian is sometimes considered snobbish. He only feels really at home in beautiful and luxurious surroundings and in the company of people of refinement and good social standing. He can, however, always appreciate anyone who has something of interest to say.

He delights in exchanging opinions with original thinkers and it is difficult for him to tolerate an uncultured or sordid environment. If the Sun is afflicted in his birth map, tolerance is one of the lessons that he has to learn.

A Leonian thrives on flattery, and praise is food for his soul. In order to do his best work he must have approbation and appreciation.

As the Sun is the ruler of Leo and the centre of the universe, so we find that Leonians invariably gravitate to positions of authority in home, government, business and the social world. In professional life they stand out from others; and no matter what their circumstances of birth, they will rise to the position for which they are fitted.

Leonians do not under-rate their own value for they are ambitious and their schemes planned on a grandiose scale. They have high ideals and far reaching aspirations.

As the Sun radiates light and warmth, so Leonians, when the Sun is unafflicted in their maps, radiate geniality and inspiration to all around them.

A Leonian is upright and strictly honourable in all his dealings. He has a fine moral character which, again if the Sun is unafflicted, makes it impossible for him to do any thing mean or petty.

More fully than people born under any other sign the Leonian is conscious of his own centre of gravity and must always work from that centre. He cannot submerge his identity in the lives of others. This is why he is frank and appreciates frankness in others.

The Leonian is lavish in expenditure. Money literally burns a hole in his pocket. Being warm hearted and generous he is often imposed upon by people who work on his feelings or pride. It is said of him that his heart is always larger than his purse.

The Leonian has a strong dramatic sense. So strongly ingrained is this quality that he is often unaware of it. In this case he will unconsciously play up to his audience, for he can always cover his deficiencies by acting a part. It is this dramatic quality which enables him to hold an audience, to tell a good story. He is interested in dramatic art and loves the theatre for he lives in the roles enacted on the stage.

Since Leo rules the heart the emotional side of life is active in a Leonian who is ardent, passionate, loyal and sincere. He has great personal magnetism and easily attracts others, so he is seldom without friends and admirers. He likes to express his love through acts of devotion and kindness and usually his affection is given to those whom he admires and in whom he can take a pride for their looks, social standing or intellectual qualities.

The Leonian takes pride in all he does for everything must reflect his own individuality. When he sets his seal on anything he takes it seriously and gives it his full attention. There is invariably something unique and distinguished about his accomplishments.

The Leonian has a quick and sometimes passionate temper but his instinct is to treat his enemies with generosity for he is naturally magnanimous.

When the Sun is afflicted Leonians become self-centred. The personal side of their life dominates and they are easily led away by their feelings. The world has a great attraction for them and among them are to be found the weakest as well as the strongest characters. Flattery leads them to a false pride and egotism; they become hard and overbearing towards inferiors, showing constant disapproval instead of giving encouragement. Sometimes they lead dissolute lives. But even so, there is something in them which helps them to rise again and to overcome their disabilities.

VIRGO ♍ (6th House)
THE VIRGIN

August 24th to September 23rd

Virgo is a mutable earth sign and ruled by Mercury. Its keyword is Service and its strongest characteristics are discrimination and criticism.

The Virgoan's attitude towards life is mental for he has a great deal of mental power and latent energy, while his mind is highly endowed and ingenious. His mentality is of the type that can be applied to action, for Virgo is the most practical sign of the Zodiac. The Virgoan is not contented with only knowing, he must *apply* what he knows.

In Gemini, the sign also ruled by Mercury, we find the intellectual type, in Virgo the intelligent type. Geminians, as a rule, profit by a good education but the intelligence of a Virgoan is more or less self-acquired.

The Virgoan is the self-taught man who accumulates knowledge through experience. His learning does not stop when he leaves school or college. Life itself is his teacher, and he has unusual powers of observation and notices things that escape the attention of others.

In fact he gives too much attention to small matters and so misses more important things. This is stressed when in the unevolved type and in all Virgoans when they are worried, for then they will be concerned with details that do not matter and neglect affairs of more importance.

The Virgoan excels in all occupations which demand attention to detail. He is the analyst, whether of chemistry or intricate machinery, and may even be the psychoanalyst. So strong is his love of the parts that he often fails to observe the whole. It is important that he should learn to understand the relationship of the parts to the whole.

Virgoans are the critics of the world for they seek true values and by comparing and observing can discover where virtue lies.

The Virgoan applies his critical faculty in all walks of life and even criticizes himself. It is perhaps his habit of self-criticism which makes him underrate his own value. His analysis of his own behaviour makes him timid, shy, retiring and afraid to take risks. In a weak map he may suffer from a feeling of inferiority.

Self-criticism renders him very sensitive to public opinion. He shuns the limelight and feels happier in a secluded place. It is not that he does not like appreciation, personal thanks and public praise; he does, but it makes him feel awkward, for he loves to give and finds it difficult to receive. He knows the joy and pleasure that comes from service and he should learn to accept graciously the service of others. The best way of expressing thanks or appreciation for his service is by a letter, which he can read alone without feeling embarrassed.

The Virgoan likes to serve a worthy cause. You may make a demand on his sympathies and get immediate help but, if you give him time to consider the matter more carefully, you may get a lecture on your own shortcomings.

His faculty for service prevents the Virgoan from being a good leader but makes him a good manager for he is industrious and persistent. He is also a good advisor and excellent business man with a quick eye for values.

The Virgoan is also an efficient salesman, but, in spite of his patience and tact, he lacks the drive which makes a good commercial traveller. The Virgoan does well in the literary world and often makes a good doctor, for he has a natural interest in diet, hygiene, nursing and medicine.

Once he can overcome his shyness the Virgoan makes an excellent teacher or lecturer. His manner is unassertive but carries a quiet conviction. His observations cover a

wide field and he excels in discussion, though he will not
express an opinion unless he has something of value to say.
He is quick to discern the weakness of his opponent's
theories and can often suggest constructive alternatives;
for, though he may lack originality, he has a gift for
improving and extending the ideas of others.

The Virgoan likes to accumulate things specially books.
He takes a lively interest in other people's affairs, can
easily adapt himself to any environment and is capable of
being all things to all men. His function is to separate the
wheat from the chaff, to criticise and to finally discard
those things and ideas which are detrimental to the community.

A Virgoan tends to shun the emotional side of life, and
specially is this the case with women, who often have a
leaning towards a professional rather than a domestic life.
This is strongly pronounced when the water element is
lacking in their maps.

The shy and retiring disposition of Virgoans is typical
of the Virgin, the symbol of Virgo. Although they are
liable to be cold in feeling yet they are not unsympathetic.
They have a quick understanding of other people's problems and can be relied upon to render service whenever
possible.

The Virgoan should learn to be less critical and more
tolerant with those who are unable to think as quickly as
he does himself. He should also try to become more aware
of other people's reactions and feelings for in this way he
will avoid giving unintentional offence and appearing self-
engrossed or selfish.

LIBRA ♎ (7th House)
THE SCALES

September 24th to October 23rd

Libra is a cardinal air sign and ruled by Venus. The key word of Libra is balance and the ideal of a Libran is to attain harmony through a state of equilibrium or inner poise. In the collective he expresses himself through his artistic activity, creating beauty in form, colour and sound.

Librans are delicately balanced. Their instinctive appreciation of this condition is revealed in their desire for peace at any price, for anger disturbs their physical harmony and interferes with the inflow of vital force.

Harmony is essential to the Libran. When it is lacking he is unable to express himself and suffers from a sense of frustration. Lack of harmony may also give rise to feelings of inferiority which, however, does not necessarily have its roots within, but may be imposed from without.

For instance, if a Libran with his artistic talents has to earn his living among business men who have no use for art he may experience a sense of inferiority. If, however, he is able to work among people who can appreciate his particular gifts he feels at home and his feeling of inferiority disappears. He should try to appreciate this point for then he will no longer be tempted to judge himself by other people's standards. Instead he will take his rightful place in the community and understand the value of the contribution he has to make to it.

Libra is represented by the Scales which for this reason have become the symbol for justice.

The Libran's sense of balance, in its positive expression, gives him the ability to weigh up intuitively, and without prejudice, opposing views, conditions and evidence, and to arrive at a just conclusion. He understands the true meaning of the word "justice" and tries to be just in all his dealings.

In its negative expression in the Libran, balance becomes instability, changing moods, indecision and the tendency to swing from one side to another without arriving at a definite conclusion. To overcome this he needs to practise concentration.

The indecision of the Libran differs from that of the Geminian. The Geminian hesitates because he can see both sides of a question at once, the Libran because he sees first one side and then another.

Libra is a social sign. It rules the seventh house and the law of association. Librans must associate in order to live fully and to develop their latent potentiality and it is fortunate that they are fond of social pleasures and amusements.

Librans are exceedingly good company. Their desire for companionship is instinctive. They find it almost impossible to live alone for they realise that they are less fortunate if they have to do this. They do their best work in partnership and are dependent upon the support of those they love and trust.

Librans often seek the company of the opposite and complementary sign, Aries, for Arians have an excess of force and self sufficiency, the qualities lacking in Librans.

Since Venus is the ruler of Libra, affections and emotions play an important part in the lives of Librans. They usually marry early, for their need to be loved is as essential to them as the air they breathe.

Librans are mentally sensitive. They shrink from anything ugly or sordid and can be thrown off their balance when their environment is inharmonious or uncongenial. They have a fine appreciation of beauty in all forms and artistic ability is marked if Venus rises or is elevated.

These people excel in any work which requires a neat touch and fine finish. They dislike any occupation which is rough and heavy or which causes them to soil their hands or clothes. They have a good dress sense and can wear their clothes well. Unless Venus is afflicted they are very orderly and cannot sit still in an untidy room. If a picture is crooked they automatically get up and straighten it.

Intuition is another outstanding quality of the Libran. This is a faculty initiated from within and higher than reason which is usually stimulated from without.

In mental expression, therefore, Librans are intuitive rather than rational. This makes them tolerant, tactful and lenient with the faults of others. But in argument this intuitive faculty can make them feel inferior since they are often unable to give reasons for their opinions and conclusions. When pressed to do so they feel at a loss in a world which knows more of reason than it does of intuition.

The male Libran is particularly prone to suffer in this way. He desires peace and appreciates gentleness, kindness, courtesy and refinement, but feels inadequate to express the more masculine qualities of aggression, physical force and driving power.

The link with higher vibrations which endows the Libran woman with grace and charm may therefore make the man appear effeminate, and so liable to suffer from a sense of inferiority. If this is so he should remember that the world has great need of these Libran qualities, particularly when they are combined with a masculine brain and outlook, for they represent a further stage of human development and are essential to the establishment of world peace and the emergence of a universal social justice.

SCORPIO ♏ *(8th House)*
THE EAGLE AND SCORPION

October 24th to November 22nd

Scorpio is a fixed water sign, and ruled by Mars. Scorpio rules the eighth house of sex, death and rebirth. It stands for sensation and feeling, generation and regeneration.

On the lower side of its nature this sign is symbolised by the Scorpion and on the higher by the Eagle. In it we find two distinct types portrayed : those who have reached the point of regeneration and those who have not yet done so.

The statement, "The greater the saint, the greater the sinner" applies marvellously well to Scorpio, for those born under its influence contain greater possibilities for either good or evil than any other. On the one hand there is the bully, the seeker after the undesirable and lower forms of sensation, cruel and masterful; on the other those whose love of sensation has been transmuted into the finer feelings and whose aspirations are directed towards the ideal of world service. At the present time some Scorpionians seem to be functioning between these two extremes.

Scorpionians are secretive, aggressive, energetic, fearless, blunt and frank, with a tendency to be sarcastic. Their temper is uncertain and they can be very quarrelsome, but as a rule they do not bear grudges.

There is a strange mixture of cowardice and courage in Scorpionians. They are strong-willed, with strong likes and dislikes towards both persons and ideas; positive in their outlook; clear, emphatic and shrewd in their judgments; firm and rather proud, with unmistakable traits of character that make them very much liked or disliked.

Scorpionians never disguise their feelings and they quickly notice the weak spots in the characters of others which they use, sometimes unscrupulously in either attack or defence. They make the best of friends and the worst and most dangerous of enemies.

Scorpionians have strong desires and are very passionate, but if they practise self-control and patience they can create within themselves a source of power which enables them to overcome all obstacles. When the best side of their nature is developed they are resourceful, courteous and kindhearted, always ready to defend the weak and helpless.

Scorpio gets its force from the planet Mars, expressing itself through the water element. It is this that makes Mars in Scorpio so different from Mars in Aries; for Aries is a fire sign and more in keeping with the Martian nature In Scorpio, however, there is a blending of two opposite elements, Fire and Water, and when these two meet uncontrolled, there is much hissing and spitting, which no doubt accounts for the unregenerate side of Scorpio. But when Fire and Water are controlled, they can create the great driving force of steam, and this represents the regenerate side of Scorpio.

Libra is the sign where we meet the law of association, and Scorpio which follows Libra denotes the results of association and so rules sexual relationships.

Scorpionians crave for sensation and seek to stimulate their feelings through new associates each of whom provides a fresh experience. For the faculty of feeling must constantly express itself through the effects we have on others and that others have on us.

Planets in Scorpio or in the eighth house denote the effect we are likely to have on other people. Thus if, in a horoscope, Saturn is found in this sign or house, the heaviness of Saturn is felt and there is a tendency for that person to have a depressing effect on others. On the other hand if Jupiter is in this position the joviality of this planet is felt and acts as an attractive force.

Undeveloped Scorpionians tend to try to escape from life instead of facing up to its problems. Scorpio rules the womb, and it seems as if they love to creep back into its warmth and darkness instead of going forward confidently to meet life. This quality shows itself in the negative expression of bullying; for if you oppose a bully, he generally slinks away.

Jealousy and suspicion are other negative traits of the Scorpionian and come from the sexual aspect of the sign. For while the Scorpionian is very exacting with others and tries to restrict their freedom, demanding purity from his partner, he himself is unwilling to be deprived of any sensation that comes his way. It is noticeable that he will often criticise and condemn others for doing the very things he likes to do himself.

A Scorpionian must learn to take his own medicine and should remember that, like the scorpion, he may sting himself if he is not careful.

The Scorpio type is strong physically although in infancy the constitution may be delicate owing to Scorpio being a water sign. The Scorpionian is magnetic and thus has a tendency to attract disease. Since Scorpio rules the house of death there is a possibility that he may lose a parent in early life.

Scorpionians are hard workers. Whatever calling they follow they pursue it whole-heartedly; for a desire for regeneration, even from the lower side of the sign, urges them to reach higher attainment.

They follow trades requiring mechanical or muscular skill or dealing with fluids. They become butchers, sailors, soldiers, engineers, brewers, and also make good doctors, surgeons, dentists, chemists or instrument makers.

Scorpionians are attracted by all forms of mystery and they are highly imaginative, because of the water element in Scorpio. They are interested in occult science for Scorpio rules death and gives a natural inclination to discover what lies behind it. Many who are authors get inspiration or bring through knowledge from planes beyond the physical.

The sensitivity of the Scorpionian to super-physical conditions endows him with a peculiar form of intuition or "knowing".

SAGITTARIUS ♐ (9th House)
THE ARCHER OR CENTAUR

November 23rd to December 22nd

Sagittarius is a mutable fire sign and ruled by Jupiter. Its symbol is the Archer, or Centaur, half horse, half man. Sagittarians have this duality, animal and human in their nature. On the one hand they love an out-door life and they excel in sports and physical culture; on the other we get the philosopher, or metaphysician who seeks to understand the deeper mysteries of life.

In olden days Sagittarius represented the priest who preached and taught the people, for this sign is ruled by Jupiter, the planet of wisdom. Today the Sagittarian is attracted to all spheres of life where wisdom does or should function: the law and everywhere where the services of an ambassador are required. He should be the Solomon of the Zodiac.

Sagittarians seem to be born with an innate understanding of what is called providence. They seldom worry about the future for they "know" that everything will turn out all right. And indeed they always seem to fall upon their feet. It is this quality which makes them optimists always full of humour, cheerfulness and encouragement.

Everyone loves their company because they are inspiring. The very presence of a true Sagittarian not only gives us strength but also a desire to carry on. He helps those weaker than himself for he is the Good Samaritan of the Bible. He has characteristics which greatly assist him: a foresight and foreknowledge which at times amounts to prophetic vision.

The Sagittarian is also strong, self-confident, self-reliant, independent, courageous, enterprising and generous. He has a high regard for truth and can sometimes give offence by being too blunt and outspoken. He calls a spade a spade and at times uses it as an agricultural instrument and so hurts others without intending to do so.

The influence of Jupiter makes the Sagittarian seek expansion. In his sports he makes international contacts. In his search for knowledge and wisdom he aims high. He shoots his arrows up into the air and cannot always see where they fall. He should be careful lest he bring condemnation on himself for failure to realise his ideals.

The Sagittarian is like an archer who should realise before he begins to shoot that many arrows will go astray before he has practised enough to hit the bulls eye with precision. The Sagittarian appears to spend the first half of his life practising, for his ideals are not usually realised until the second half of life. Before he shoots the arrow of his idea into the air he should always have a goal in view as this will attract his arrows to the bulls eye and bring success to his schemes. When he has learnt to achieve direction and purpose he can accomplish great things.

The Sagittarian is sometimes called a hypocrite. For his dual nature makes him fluctuate between the abstract and the concrete worlds. He may live an inner life which is hardly revealed at all. Hence he is difficult to understand. He may be known to one group of friends as interested in philosophy, religion or metaphysics, while his acquaintances in the public house will know him as a good natured humorous companion. In the one group he is appreciated for his good judgment and depth of thought; in the other for his sportsmanlike qualities. The Sagittarian however is not a hypocrite. The truth is that he can live in two different worlds and feel quite at home in either.

The symbolism of Sagittarius suggests that the transition from horse to man is realised in the change from the animal consciousness of youth to the more abstract consciousness of the mature man. A Sagittarian can do much to link these two worlds and to lead others to states of consciousness beyond the physical.

The Sagittarian desires to travel both mentally and physically. He is interested in foreign affairs, shipping and geographical pursuits.

In all his dealing the Sagittarian is sincere, honest and trustworthy. If Jupiter is afflicted he will be irresponsible; one who talks much and accomplishes little. In this case he should learn to listen to other peoples' opinions or he will become a good-natured bore.

The Sagittarian responding to the positive influence of the sign is capable of deep devotion to a cause or ideal. He has a deep religious sense for he knows instinctively that man is not self-created but is a part of a greater whole. And to the creative powers of the Universe he desires to give thanks.

CAPRICORN ♑ *(10th House)*

THE SEA-GOAT AND SCAPEGOAT

December 23rd to January 20th

Capricorn is a cardinal earth sign ruled by the planet Saturn. It is symbolised by the Goat and Capricornians have many of its characteristics; being quiet and steady, cautious and sure-footed, they seek to go from one mountain peak to another, alone and unaided; in life they climb by their own efforts.

Capricornians are cold and calculating, lack cheerfulness and are subject to despondent moods. They are at times inclined to look too much on the darker side of things. But in spite of this Capricorn is a strong sign. Those born under it are ambitious, persevering, prudent, economical, very patient and careful.

Capricornians are deep thinkers, with an honest nature, and a great love of justice. They aim at perfection and are not easily turned aside in anything they have undertaken. They like responsibility and large undertakings and, because of their outstanding practical organising and executive ability, they generally succeed.

They are hard workers and can carry on for a long time without being discouraged. This is fortunate for they often meet with opposition which they strive to overcome with tact and diplomacy. They seldom make a direct attack but prefer to find a way round an obstacle. Although at times fate seems to be against them they can usually make the most of their opportunities.

They are not over-generous for they feel that everything should be earned. They do not make friends easily, yet they are faithful in their friendships, which are sometimes of a secret nature. They make unrelenting enemies. They respect old age and are fond of ancient customs and antiques.

It appears that one of the functions of a Capricornian is to bring to earth the arrows of ideas and aspirations shot into the air by Sagittarius. A Capricornian always has his feet firmly planted on the ground. He manages the things of the earth; for Capricorn placed at the cardinal point of the tenth house where we meet the collective, rules the governments of the world.

The wisdom and knowledge gained in Sagittarius has to be applied in a practical manner, and the Capricornian feels this responsibility heavily : hence his seriousness and his feelings of weight and depression when things go wrong. He is troubled not only by personal difficulties but is strongly affected by political and world events, and in these moods he is pessimistic and doubts his own ability.

When a Capricornian is responding to the positive side of the sign he is ambitious and, as he has a strong sense of duty and a desire to pull his weight in the community, he feels he must do something to help solve its problems. This is a typically Saturnian ambition, demanding that the effort be self-induced and carried through in a slow, practical way, until he can take command and do something to improve existing conditions.

But when they are functioning on the personal side of life Capricornians should be very careful how they use their power. If they over-reach themselves their urge for power may get beyond control and become very destructive. For the higher they go, the giddier they may become. They see things in a wrong perspective and, at the next jump, may lose their foothold and great may be their fall.

The spirit of Capricorn seems to be in the Scottish race, because so many Scots have left their country and climbed to positions of responsibility in other parts of the world.

This ability to rise in life, so characteristic of the Capricornian, depends to a great extent upon the position of Saturn in the map. When Saturn is strongly placed and well aspected, then all the positive qualities of Capricorn such as perseverance, ambition, self-reliance, calmness, deliberation, will come to the fore. But when Saturn is afflicted, then the negative qualities of this sign, such as suspicion, self-centredness, conceit, narrowness, fear of being cheated, slandered, or oppressed will be apparent.

Too much concentration on one thing makes a Capricornian one-sided. To avoid this, he should associate more and learn to exchange ideas freely in order to get a broader vision of life.

He should also guard against belittling the ideas of other people, try to be more demonstrative, and show his sympathy more freely. The Capricornian finds it difficult to be appreciative in personal relationships. This is probably because he likes to exercise authority over others, but it makes him appear cold, and if he persists in this attitude and fails to give generous praise where it is due, he may suffer from feelings of loneliness and isolation.

Another great trial to the Capricornian is his fear of insecurity. There is a tendency that he may spoil his life by the urgency of his desire to make provision for his old age. He should learn to live more fully in the "now", in order that he may have more experiences to assimilate and consider in his old age. He usually lives long.

The life expression of a Capricornian is through the material world, and he strives to make his ideals concrete but, as he prefers action to promises, he is always striving after effects. He excels as a manager or organiser, and is capable of carrying responsibility unless Saturn is afflicted, when he shuns it.

Capricornians follow occupations connected with the earth, e.g. farming, estate work or mining. They are attracted to politics and local government and do well in the business world. If Venus is well aspected they make good architects. In whatever they undertake they can be trusted not to act impulsively but to plod on until their work is brought to a successful conclusion.

AQUARIUS ≈ (11th House)
THE WATER-BEARER

January 21st to February 19th

Aquarius is a fixed air sign. Its old ruler is Saturn. But Uranus, whose orbit lies beyond that of Saturn, has, since its discovery, been considered to be a second ruler. The influence of Uranus is responsible for the new type of man who will appear on the earth and many of those born under the sign of Aquarius are responsive to it.

Freedom and altruism are keynotes of Aquarius. Aquarians make their own way in life and think out their own moral code. They do things in an individual fashion and seek freedom for others as well as for themselves.

An Aquarian thinks in terms of the future. He looks forward to the time when man will come into his birthright and the material essentials for life (food, clothing, shelter) will be guaranteed to all.

The Aquarian has a sub-conscious urge to make the earth a better place for man to live in. He understands that Nature has supplied a superabundance and that it is man himself who has created an artificial and clumsy system of distribution. He seeks therefore to make people aware that the faults of the present system lie with man and not with nature.

This makes an Aquarian take an interest in science, not so much for its own sake as in the conviction that through the application of scientific inventions the burden of everyday life may be lightened. He tries to understand spiritual as well as physical science, and in the workings of natural law he recognises the workings of a Universal Mind.

The Aquarian is essentially a humanitarian and belongs to those who will make the ideal of world citizenship a practical reality. He knows little or nothing of the word "stranger". To him all men are friends with whom he can associate freely because he has the power to sense the unique human quality which lies beneath all outward differences of colour, race or caste.

The Aquarian is thus a good judge of human nature. But while he can understand others, he himself is often misjudged. For he is a revolutionary, always wanting to change the old for the new.

His quality of humanitarianism makes the Aquarian appreciate the small amenities of life. He realises, for instance, that his morning coffee is due to the service of many others who are working to supply his needs. He appreciates the ease with which it is produced, and the fact that he does not have to bother about the cultivation of the beans, their transportation, roasting, grinding and even delivery to his door.

Again, his humanitarianism makes him appear detached and impersonal. Even in love he cannot be exclusive, for although he may love one person in all sincerity, yet he cannot for this reason exclude the rest of the world from his affection. He feels that the human race is one big family, and he loves it. Thus his love has a universal quality and the Aquarian is always ready to be of service to those who need help.

We have said that Aquarius is a fixed sign. Where then is the fixity? It is expressed in the Aquarian's purposes and opinions. It is a fixity within his own individual centre. Thinking in terms of his relationship to all around him, he never loses himself nor does he seek to merge his identity with that of another.

It is a strange type of fixity which is coupled with the changeability of Uranus. The Aquarian feels himself to be at the axis of the wheel as well as on its circumference. Thus he is aware that if he is to succeed in introducing a new world order, his purpose to do so must remain steady, and he must know exactly where he stands in relation to the collective.

The Aquarian can keep his purposefulness and tranquillity in the most trying circumstances, because he thinks not only in terms of the present but of the present in relation to the past and the future. His urge to live in the future drives him to investigate conditions beyond the plane of physical consciousness. While he is the mystic who can see God in the flower, he is also the occultist who tries to understand how God made it.

The above is a description of an Aquarian who responds positively to the influence of Uranus. But when in a birth map Uranus is inharmoniously aspected to other planets, then the Aquarian's expression becomes more negative. Although the Uranian force is still present he will use it for self-aggrandisement. His attitude will then be : "What does the future hold for *me*?" He will work for reforms to gain publicity for himself. He has not grasped the idea of wholeness, and an element of selfishness creeps in.

Or, again, when the force of Uranus is repressed the Aquarian may become eccentric, liable to sudden explosions and so uncertain in his manner that he is at a loss to explain his own actions. In these circumstances it is impossible for his associates to predict what his next move will be. This uncertainty and eccentricity, however has nothing whatever to do with insanity. It is simply the Uranian force seeking to be manifested without inner direction or control.

A quite different quality is found in Aquarians who have not yet transmuted the Saturnian vibration into the Uranian. These people are not yet defined out of the whole and so are still under the influence of Saturn. The only way they can develop their individuality and become aware of themselves is through being self-centred.

The selfishness of the Saturn Aquarian is manifested through such qualities as determination, patience, perseverance, decided opinions and strong likes and dislikes. These people are cautious, steady and practical. Their fixity takes the form of adherence to old traditions and the established order, in which they feel at home and sure of themselves. They resist what is new and strange because it presents a problem demanding readjustment before it can be assimilated and made part of themselves.

The influence of Saturn as the builder of forms shows itself also in their reliance on possessions, and in the comparisons which they make between their own position and that of others. They are sceptical of anything which they cannot apply to their own experience.

In the sign of Aquarius we get the transmutation from selfishness to altruism. Under the sign of Aquarius the new man is born. At the present time the majority of those born under this sign are in the transitional stage, fluctuating between the Saturnian and Uranian vibrations. This is the period when the "old man" is dying and the "new man" is not yet born.

PISCES ♓ (12th House)
THE FISHES OR FISHERMAN

February 20th to March 20th

Pisces is a mutable water sign ruled by Jupiter. The chief characteristics of Pisceans are sensitivity, and emotional response; thus feeling, emotion and sensation play an important part in their lives.

Positively, the Piscean qualities are expressed in warmth of heart, sympathy, compassion, understanding and a rather mystical attitude towards life. The sympathies of the Piscean are all-embracing and extended to animals as well as human beings so that all who suffer, sorrow or who are in any way afflicted, always find comfort and consolation in their presence.

Pisceans are naturally quiet, trustful, loving, courteous and hospitable. They have high ideals and a fertile imagination. They can sense an atmosphere and when they find themselves in an uncongenial environment they are easily cast down and made despondent.

Pisceans have an intense desire to merge themselves with the thoughts and feelings of others. They like to co-operate mentally, emotionally, and physically with all that is going on around them, and so are readily absorbed into any social movement which has compassion for its ideal.

The Piscean sensitivity to the thoughts and feelings of other people is a great and valuable gift provided it is used wisely and with discretion. When carried to extremes it can be harmful, for it leads to a diffusion of energy and hinders satisfactory function. The Piscean should learn to bring reason to bear on his emotions and so to become more conscious of himself and his own centre of gravity.

It is important, too, that he should try to distinguish

between his own emotional reactions and those which he may pick up from others, for if he identifies himself too much with other people's lives he may lose his own way in life.

(I have met negative Pisceans with sympathies so over-developed that they did nothing but complain and even rebelled against God for allowing suffering in the world. Such people can neither enjoy their own blessings nor fulfil their own potentiality.)

When a Piscean loses himself in this way he soon begins to feel frustrated and so takes on the condition of a martyr which, in some cases, he even enjoys. When he can no longer enjoy his own sufferings he indulges in self-pity and forgets, that he has a duty to the collective.

Pisceans are sometimes accused of day-dreaming and of laziness. This may be either because they have lost their own centre of gravity or because their psychic sensitivity distracts their attention from the things of everyday life.

Most Pisceans experience a desire to escape from reality, which negatively makes them unpractical day dreamers but which when used positively can be a valuable asset. The intuitive faculties of the Piscean are highly developed and if he can transform his faculty for day-dreaming into that of creative imagination he can bring through from the unseen worlds ideas which are of great value not only to himself but to the world in general. In order to accomplish this the Piscean should guard against negative emotionalism and maintain a positive attitude towards life.

The Piscean who is functioning satisfactorily pays great attention to the neatness of his dress and is quick to notice any outward deficiencies on the part of others. The world of beauty in sound, colour, and form takes on greater significance; and the sense of unworthiness, which arises from a consciousness of his own imperfections, will disappear as he takes his rightful place in the community.

Pisceans should study the story of Cinderella, from which they can learn a great deal. Cinderella in the kitchen portrays those who have not yet learnt to find themselves, whose thoughts are without direction and swayed by passing emotions; Cinderella as a princess, those who have found their own centre of gravity and whose thoughts and emotions initiated from within, are manifested as blessings to all.

PHYSICAL CHARACTERISTICS OF THE SIGNS

The Rising Sign is of great importance in delineation. When the time of birth is unknown one of the ways in which it may be determined is by the physical characteristics and general appearance of the person. Many factors are involved. The rising planets and the sign in which the Sun, Moon and Ruler are placed all tend to modify the physical appearance. The ruler of the rising decanate is also important if it is prominently placed in the horoscope.

Some Rising Signs throw the characteristics of their polar opposites. This is often the case with the Cardinal signs. Aries or Capricorn rising, for instance may give the appearance of Libra or Cancer and considerable experience is needed to recognise this interchange. Aquarius and Leo can be mistaken for one another. Many Aquarians have a tawny leonine look resembling the statues in the Vatican in which Mithra is depicted as a man with the head of a lion.

Gemini-Sagittarius, Pisces-Virgo, Taurus-Scorpio on the other hand are less often confused with one another.

Fire signs rising give a tendency to baldness. The Hair is thin and recedes from the temples in early life. Water and earth signs, with the exception of Capricorn, give a tendency to corpulence.

The sign on the cusp of the fourth house modifies the physical appearance in old age and after middle life.

ARIES. Pointed face and sharp chin. Wiry, tense body. Walks with a springy step and rather delicately. Taps his foot to music or when impatient. Bushy eyebrows. Tendency to stroke the back of the head.

TAURUS. Broad shoulders, narrow hips. Short thick neck,

heavy lower jaw. Soft curly hair. Deep chested. Eyes cow-like or small and dangerous like those of the bull. Has a habit of stroking or holding his throat and looks at you with his forehead! The prize fighter and the opera singer are typical examples of this sign.

GEMINI.   Tall slender body. Walks with quick short steps and with stiff hips. Long restless hands and fingers. Gesticulates with his hands. Alert nervous manner. Bright quick eye. Walks up and down when thinking.

CANCER.   Soft body large in proportion to short arms and legs, small hands and feet in first and second decanates. Twists feet together or round the legs of a chair. Has habit of putting one arm behind his back and grasping the other elbow. Goes upstairs sideways. Feet slightly turned inward. Body hunched sideways when thinking or in old age. Eyes prominent, protruding on stalks like those of a crab.

LEO.   Upright dignified carriage. Royal bearing. Walks well. Eye large and well opened or small and twinkling; often light in colour. Sometimes has a prowling feline movement and walks on the balls of his feet. Places hand on heart when talking and expressing emotion.

VIRGO.   Long stiff body. Large stomach in later life. Square hands. Hair grows to a widow's peak. Forehead slopes backwards and is often low in a female. Habit of holding hands on stomach. If Mercury is afflicted fidgets with fingers and toes. Bushy eyebrows.

LIBRA.   Body usually well proportioned and neat. Good balance. Walks well and moves gracefully unless Venus is afflicted. Heart-shaped face. Inclined to stoutness in later life. Male has a feminine look. Sometimes a small mouth unless Venus is placed in a strong sign where it may considerably modify the Libran appearance.

SCORPIO. Body thick set and muscular. Arms and legs long. Legs shapely and well developed sometimes slightly bow shaped. Prominent brows, "beetling". Roman nose. The "Scorpio eye", penetrating and with drooping lids. Rubs or strokes nose.

SAGITTARIUS. Tall, loose body with long arms and legs. Movements unco-ordinated if Mercury or Jupiter are afflicted. Colt-like appearance in adolescence. Long stride. Horsy sloping shoulders, wide hips. Women often have saddle back. Inclined to stoop from shoulders. Female often has thick thighs and legs.

CAPRICORN. Spare bony body with large knee, wrist and finger joints. Knobbly knees. Bony forehead. Body inclined forward from waist. Seldom looks you straight in the eye. Glance shifts from one thing to another. Long neck. Thin ears. Teeth set in narrow jaw and often discoloured. Eye opaque and lack-lustre or round, bright and clear like that of a goat.

AQUARIUS. Two distinct types are born under this sign, the Saturnian and the Uranian. Both have well-formed bodies but the Saturnian is sparse and smaller, the Uranian larger and fuller with bigger bones and less prominent joints. Teeth excellent unless ruler is afflicted. Legs and ankles often thick and malformed. Direct, fearless glance. The "Aquarian Eye" detached and impersonal. Does not change its expression either in happiness or anger. Appears to be fixed on a distant object or to behold a vision.

PISCES. Body has indefinite outline. May be either large or small but is always soft and flabby. Hands and feet large in first and third decanates, smaller in the second. Face round and sometimes flattened. Feet turn outwards like a fishes tail. Rolling gait, often clumsy in movement. The "Fish Eye" prominent, full and watery, often pale in colour. Sometimes a receding chin.

PHYSICAL CHARACTERISTICS OF THE PLANETS

SUN. Tall strong body. Large head. High rounded forehead. Hair inclined to be thin and to recede from temples. Dignified appearance.

MOON. Plump body inclined to stoutness. Round face, pale skin, grey eyes. Soft abundant hair.

MERCURY. Tall slender upright body. Long face. High forehead. Long straight or slightly curved nose. Thin lips. Hair plentiful. Long limbs. Quick and active.

VENUS. Well proportioned rather small body. Round cheeks. Good clear complexion. dimpled smiling face. Musical voice.

MARS. Strong muscular well-set body. Well covered but not stout. Sharp piercing eyes. Roman nose.

JUPITER. Above average height. Upstanding. Plump. Plentiful hair. Oval face. High forehead, fresh complexion. Handsome.

SATURN. Lean face and body. Small dark eyes deeply set. Pale complexion. Dark Saturnine look. Lean or ill formed legs and bad gait.

URANUS. Tall, above average height, with large bones. Features strongly marked. Square face.

NEPTUNE. If rising a luminous skin and a look of "otherness". Face usually pale and sensitive. A dreamy visionary look which sets him apart. A changeling.

URANUS THE AWAKENER

*A lecture delivered to the Astrologer's
Convention at Harrogate in April, 1941*

In my lecture last year we linked Man with the Solar
System and studied the unfoldment of the human life
cycle, dealing with those planets whose orbits lie within
that of Saturn.

A short resumé of how response to these planets within
the boundary set by Saturn transformed Animal Man into
Human Man will help us to understand the function of
Uranus in connection with the next evolutionary step of
the human race.

The function of Saturn is to bring Man from a state of
unawareness to that of awareness and to define us out of
the whole.

In those far-off days when man was little more than an
animal, his body was coarse and heavy and his response to
external stimulus slight. He was, as yet, functioning within
the human group soul and so unaware of himself as a
separate unit in the Universe.

At this time, Saturn played the leading role in human
evolution was the first planet to evoke human response
and to direct the emergence of the first crude human
forms.

The function of Saturn was not only to define man at
the physical level but also to relate him to the earth—to
reveal to him the nature of the planet on which he lived,
to teach him that the earth sustained him and gave forth
fruit in order that he himself might survive.

After long ages the human form became less heavy and
as its vibratory rate increased men at last began to
respond to the vibrations of Jupiter.

It is then that we can discern the beginnings of social life, the emergence of leaders; a form of elementary priest-craft—in short the dawn of response to something other than the earth.

Those who were responsive to the influence of Jupiter became the leaders of the herd; the first religious conceptions grew from their efforts to teach others what they themselves had been able to apprehend.

When, still later, man became responsive to the influence of the next planet, Mars, war, strife, and discord disrupted community life, for the impact of desire and aggression on primitive man must have caused a great upheaval.

For the first time man felt the lust for power and the desire to subjugate others weaker than himself. His increased strength stimulated his taste for adventure and urged him to explore his surroundings and seek to conquer other tribes. Weapons were invented, physical desires intensified as the body became warmer and the blood flowed more quickly.

The negative or destructive qualities of Mars were, no doubt, evident at this time so the greatest honour and highest place belonged by right to the strongest and most powerful.

The Dawn of Affection

In time as human response quickened man became responsive to the vibrations of Venus. Then he felt within himself strange stirrings and vague feelings whose nature he did not understand but which were intensified when he approached his mate. Through a growing tenderness and gentleness he realised at last the possibility of something more than physical passion, lust and sex. Men and women felt a growing attraction towards certain individuals. Instead of mating more or less indiscriminately within the tribe they selected their mates with greater care.

The search for ways and means to express a growing

emotion and affection led to the evolution of art and music. Man began to decorate his dwellings and his body; to take an interest in sounds and their combinations. When, in course of time, the more progressive became responsive to the Mercurial vibrations the early forms of culture were already established.

Then evolution was speeded up. With the dawn of mental faculties man began to make comparisons and to discriminate between one idea and another. The faculty of reasoning was slowly developed together with a clearer expression in speech and perhaps a rude attempt to record past experiences and events in symbols.

At this stage the human physical body resembled that of present day man. Since then, through response to the combined influences of Saturn, Jupiter, Mars, Venus and Mercury, Man has established a link with the Solar System and so has developed into what he is today. For with those planets that lie within the orbit of Saturn we have the story of the unfoldment of human potentiality from Animal Man to Human Man. But life is subject to the law of continuity. Each goal attained reveals a further horizon.

Man has now to become responsive to those planets which lie *beyond* the orbit of Saturn—Uranus, Neptune, Pluto. We are now established as human beings but by the law of continuity we must make still greater progress. We must struggle from the state of Human Man to that of God Man.

Uranus, the Great Awakener, who now takes the place of Saturn as teacher and guide of mankind, urges us forward to states of greater awareness. The keyword of Uranus is altruism and it is altruism that Uranus will bring into creative function in the human race.

Not until the human mind had become sufficiently responsive to the vibrations of Mercury was man able to "tune in" to those of Uranus and to respond to those new impulses which fired him with a desire for freedom and independence. It is significant that the French and Amer-

ican Revolutions occurred almost immediately after the
discovery of Uranus.

Riots, strikes, unrest and other disturbances followed for
the old way of life had to be broken down to make way
for the new.

The Machine Age

So, response to the influence of Uranus introduced the
Machine Age and increased the speed of production. Men
became so engrossed in production that they overlooked
the fact that goods have a consumer's as well as a pro-
ducer's value. This human misconception retarded progress and deprived the world of the benefits it should have
received from Uranus. Many Uranian inventions are even
now lying on the shelves of the Patent Office; others have
been bought up by this or that company in order to maintain a high rate of interest.

Uranus was discovered in 1781. Its first orbital journey
round the Sun, completed in 1865, can be considered as a
transition period in which the ground was broken up and
prepared for the second journey, when the seeds of
altruism began to sprout and the action of Uranus was
more thorough and far-reaching in its effects. The second
orbital journey of Uranus will be completed in 1949, and
in the last eighty years changes of great magnitude have
taken place in every field of human endeavour.

It would appear that Uranus has a greater influence on
the other planets than they have on each other. If, for
instance, we examine the influence of Uranus on Saturn
we shall see how agriculture has been revolutionised. Look
also at the effect on architecture—buildings designed to
express their function, the labour-saving devices and
improved constructional methods of modern building.

Now turn to the effect of the Uranian influence on
Jupiter and see how it has broken down the old restricting
ways of life, how the clergy have had to renounce their
narrow teaching of brimstone and fire, how the vision of

life has broadened, how we are now beginning to understand something of the creative power of thought and to know that within us is the power.

It is easy, too, to see the effect of this influence on Mars, for the present war differs greatly from any other. Perhaps here the altruism of Uranus is not so pleasant, for truly this is everybody's war. We know, however, that this great conflict is a part of the labour pangs which will bring new conditions to birth. Now that Uranus has taken over the reins from Saturn, life is speeded up, for Uranus can accomplish more in twenty years that Saturn in a hundred.

Modern Warfare

Modern warfare bears many characteristics of Uranus, who uses old things in new ways, is inventive, destructive, revolutionary, and has an entirely new set of values.

The effect of the Uranian influence on Venus is already evident in the arts. We now have jazz and swing music and what is known as the modern school of painting. We are living, however, in a transition period when the old and the new ideas of art are in conflict. In the coming Age of Aquarius all forms of artistic expression will be revolutionised, but those who will give full expression to the new forms and who will be the masters of the future in these subjects are not yet born.

The effect of the Uranian influence on Mercury has radically altered our ideas about education. State schools and compulsory education are now a feature common in many countries. In every part of the world there is a growing demand for increased educational facilities. In this country, scholarships and free libraries provide everyone with opportunity for self-development and the pursuit of literary tastes.

Uranus has the power to transfigure everything it touches. When this planet entered the sign of Aries some fourteen years ago significant events occurred which have been instrumental in breaking down the old order. Then new ideas of leadership emerged; the egotism and martial qualities of Aries were expressed in a new form of dictatorship.

But the impact of the Uranian power intoxicated the dictators and caused them to go to extremes which will prove to be their undoing. It will not be until children born with Uranus in Aries are old enough to take their place in the world that this form of Uranian influence will be fully expressed and appreciated by the world at large. It will be the children born between January 13th, 1928 and March 29th, 1935 who, having the true spirit of altruism in their make-up, will introduce the new forms of administration. They will be the pioneers of the new age and will establish a new order among men.

Uranus is at present (1941) in Taurus and it is evident that the old financial system in which altruism had no place is now tottering. We get a shadow of things to come in the "Lease and Lend" Bill which, although the greatest financial transaction that has ever taken place, is not subject to the old laws. The aim of Uranus is security for all. But here again the new financial system will not be established until children born while Uranus is in Taurus are old enough to introduce it. These children will have a unique grasp of monetary problems and will surely solve them in a surprising and altruistic fashion.

Educational Reform

Uranus is now moving towards the sign of Gemini and in the seven years from 1942 to 1949 we shall see many educational reforms. In its first orbital journey, Uranus made it possible for everyone to learn how to read and write. This time faculties for the higher forms of education will be made available for all who can benefit from them, irrespective of their status of birth or their ability to pay. The "old school tie" has lost its power. Children born in the next seven years will revolutionise existing educational ideas and, when they are grown up, it is they who will have the vision to understand the true meaning of education and the right of every child to the best that can be provided.

Uranus will also give us new systems of communications—convert long into short journeys. Science will seek in the realm of metaphysics the solutions of problems which can no longer be related to physical phenomena. At the same time the mind of the average man will expand and begin to grasp something of the greater Cosmic laws.

If we had more time at our disposal we could follow the path of Uranus round the Zodiac and trace with confidence the varying effects of the Great Awakener in all fields of human endeavour.

We have studied something of the effects of the Uranian influence at the physical level. We must not forget, however, that the main influence of Uranus is psychological and is destined to awaken faculties which will develop the God within each one of us.

Before the human race became responsive to the Uranian vibrations, man was content to follow the line of least resistance, and the majority were only too content to allow others to do their thinking for them.

But since the mission of Uranus is with the many and not the few this condition now has to cease. The desire for freedom and liberty grew apace and men everywhere began to awaken to the inner or subjective realities of life.

In recent years much has been written and published about individuality, the individual and the process of individuation. Many have taken great interest in the study of the mind and mental processes generally. The wider spread of esoteric knowledge has helped in many ways to release man's latent potentiality and to give him a more comprehensive and spiritual idea of the cosmos.

Indeed the consciousness of man has so greatly expanded that he is now beginning to think in terms of universal citizenship and world-government

The Uranian influence has affected the governments of all countries. Even Germany will become subservient to the New Order of Man which Uranus is now seeking to establish on the earth. No power on earth, no group or body of men can repress the great awakening which lies before the human race.

It has been the function of Saturn to bring man to a condition of awareness when Uranus could endow him with power to overcome all obstacles and to create necessities and even luxuries at the physical level. Much has already been accomplished. Man is now released from long hours of labour and has leisure to develop himself and to establish a new culture in which the development of beauty and art take first place.

The Next Step

Our next step is to further expand the mind and mental functions, for in no other way can the illusions, superstitions and outworn traditions be destroyed. Man has lived in bondage for long ages but now, through the influence of Uranus men and women are seeing things in a new light.

It is Uranus who helps us to get out of the herd and to stand on our own feet. But when we do this we become exiles. The world of yesterday did not understand Uranians. The very people who poured their thought creations into the aura of this earth and so brought about better conditions for the herd were often condemned as cranks or unpractical visionaries. For he who gets out of the herd and begins to think for himself, becomes responsible for the herd, and has to serve it to the best of his ability.

At first these Uranian exiles were very few but every day their number increases and when exile joins hand with exile a new order of man is made.

If you study the lives of those who have the Sun in benefic aspect to Uranus at birth, you will find that they always attract people who will help them so that they are never alone and are frequently the centre of a group. When they are in difficulties, at the psychological moment, someone turns up who can give them the assistance or guidance they need.

The reverse is the case with those who have negative Sun-Uranus aspects. These people are learning how to find their own centre of gravity. They are thrown on their own resources and frequently suffer from loneliness and a sense of frustration. These conditions are necessary before they can become fully aware of themselves and capable of acting independently.

No doubt this is the reason why the negative aspects of Uranus to both Sun and Moon are known as "separative" aspects, which even break the marriage tie lest that person should lose himself in the life of another. Uranus will not accept us until we have broken the bonds and learned the lessons that Saturn and the planets within its boundary have to teach us. Response to Uranus, the guardian of those planets which lie beyond Saturn, gives us the strength to get out of the herd and in time to become responsible for it. For, until we have learnt all there is to learn in the journey from Animal Man to Human Man, Uranus cannot awaken our response to states of awareness which lie beyond the three dimensional plane.

The more quickly we are able to "tune in" to the vibratory rate of Uranus and the superphysical planes, the more quickly shall we discover the secrets of nature's hidden forces and the way in which their power can be harnessed in the service of humanity. Electricity as a means of light and heat will soon be out-dated and it is probable that through a greater understanding of the laws of gravity new modes of travel and transport will be introduced. Added to this scientists are now rapidly approaching the time when they will have to explore the metaphysical realm in order to find a satisfactory solution to many of the problems which now confront them.

Uranus and Astrology

Let us consider Uranus in relation to the "language of

the Gods"—Astrology. In the past Saturn and Jupiter were the planets which indicated the more progressive men of the race who studied and tried to understand the working of natural law. Today it is from Uranus that we seek enlightenment for it is Uranus alone who can rupture the bonds set by Saturn and lead us towards the new worlds we have to conquer.

I have been asked on many occasions how the old astrologers managed without Uranus. It is, however, easy to see that they had no need of this planet for the things represented by Uranus are those which response to Uranus has introduced. Before we were able to "tune in" to Uranus the things of Uranus did not exist.

But today the position is different. The majority of men are responsive to Uranus in greater or lesser degree and so are able to take part in the great procession that is moving towards Aquarius. Uranus is known as the Astrological planet and years ago I said that when Uranus entered the sign of Aries there would be a revival of Astrology.

It is not surprising that in its initial stages this revival has taken a popular and elementary form, for Uranus deals not with the few but with the many and seeks to bring astrology to the notice of the greatest number of people in the shortest possible time. Hence we have had newspaper predictions, magazine articles, and even talks on the American radio.

When in 1952, Uranus moves into Gemini the deeper and more scientific approach will come to the fore and many serious minded people will begin to take an interest in the subject.

It is through response to the Uranian vibrations that we shall gain a deeper insight into astrological laws and a greater understanding not only of the Solar System itself but also of those great forces which influence it from without—the constellations of the Great Bear and the Pleiades, the great Star Sirius and the Seven Solar Systems of which our own is a member.

For Astrology, as all astrologers know, is still in its

infancy. There is so much that is hidden from us, so much that we do not understand. We must look to the influence of Uranus, Neptune and Pluto to help us to "think through" this greater knowledge which we so earnestly desire to possess.

How little we know about the vibrations of our own planet, the earth. We are as ignorant of the way in which we are affected by them as we are of their effect on the Solar System as a whole.

We can see what extraordinary progress has been made in the world since the discovery of Uranus. A profound change has taken place on the earth and in the minds of men—a change which must surely be registered in the Solar System and so have an effect on the other planets. We can surmise, too, that Uranus has affected the other planets and stimulated their evolution. Such factors will have to be taken into account, for Astrology, like everything else is subject to the law of Continuity. Our understanding of its laws must progress year by year and age by age.

Ancient Text Books

If we examine the text books of Lilly. Gadbury and Ramesey published between 1647 and 1653 we shall find delineations of aspects to Mars and Saturn which today we are unable to accept.

Ramesey, in relation to people born under Mars, uses such terms as "murderous and cut-throat people"; James Wilson writing as recently as 1819 says that the real disposition of those born under Mars consists of these qualities—"anger, violence, and an eager wish to be in quarrels and mischief. The countenance is extremely vicious and unbending, rude, unkind, ferocious and bitter."

There is no mention among these early astrological writers of the constructive aspect of the Martian energy. It is evident today, that Mars no longer exerts a negative influence on us. This is because Mars has also evolved and its force is becoming more constructive.

Similar conditions apply, of course, to all planets. So that from time to time Astrologers will have to revise their findings in accordance with changes taking place within the Solar System.

Many other changes which provide evidence of evolution within the Solar System can also be discerned. Astrologers of the fifteenth and sixteenth centuries, for instance, commonly used orbs of influence extending as far as fourteen and even fifteen degrees. Today because of the increased sensitivity of the human soul we use orbs of only six to eight degrees.

Similarly, the modern astrologer finds that many of the systems and devices in vogue two or three hundred years ago are no longer valid. The reason is that we are no longer subject to them for they represent a phase which has been out-lived.

It would, I think, be as well for us to understand that the vibratory rate of the earth affects the whole Solar System. Since at this time the earth is becoming responsive to the influence of Aquarius and the human vibratory rate being stepped up all the other planets will have a share in the new experiences that await us in the coming age of Aquarius.

If anyone should feel that the evolutionary process outlined in this lecture appears to contradict what is known about the development of the great civilizations of the past, the answer is as follows :—

In that far distant time when man was first beginning to become responsive to the Mercurial vibrations, the human mind existed in embryonic form only—its potentiality was latent, but not yet actual.

The Planetary Hierarchy was therefore unable to contact man on the mental plane and in order to stimulate the growth and establishment of mental faculties, it was necessary for them to come to earth and live in physical contact with the human race.

The great civilizations of the past were, therefore, the result of Hierarchial activities and so cannot be considered as examples of independent human effort.

When, at last, after long ages, the human mind became sufficiently established to function independently on the mental plane the Hierarchy withdrew and left man to work out his own salvation. Had they not done so, their continued physical presence would have retarded, rather than accelerated, human progress.

During their sojourn on earth, members of the Planetary Hierarchy taught men many things. After their withdrawal from the physical world much of their teaching faded from human memory and now has to be rediscovered through man's own endeavour and experiment.